D1571995

TEMPORARY

DWELLINGS

Temporary Dwellings
Phyllis Janowitz

UNIVERSITY OF PITTSBURGH PRESS

Published by the University of Pittsburgh Press, Pittsburgh, Pa. 15260
Feffer and Simons, Inc., London
Manufactured in the United States of America

Library of Congress Cataloging in Publication Data

Janowitz, Phyllis.
   Temporary dwellings.

   (Pitt poetry series)
   I. Title.   II. Series.
PS3560.A534T4   1987   811'.54   87-40221
ISBN 0-8229-3566-X
ISBN 0-8229-5394-3 (pbk.)

The author and publisher wish to express their grateful acknowledgment to the following publications in which some of these poems first appeared: *Backbone* ("Anthropology"); *Barnwood* ("Thin as a Nickel, Edgeless," published under the title "Mother"); *Boston Review* ("Cole Porter Has a Nervous Breakdown," "The Hotel Plus La Même Chose," and "My Mother's Cruise"); *Boulevard* ("Keepers of the Flame"); *Bound* ("The Small Loaf of the Artist in Society"); *Chiaroscuro* ("Composition of a Windy Knight" and "Washed Up with Maxwell Bodenheim"); *Connections* ("Perspective in Gray and Green"); *Ecstatic Occasions, Expedient Forms* ("Change"); *Epoch* ("Little Elegy," "Orpheus and *La Dolce Vita*," "Voices," and "What We Know About Right-Angled Triangles"); *Image* ("Pâté"); *Ithaca Women's Anthology #7* ("Fat Lena & Mr. M." and "My Sister"); *Ithaca Women's Anthology #9* ("Change" and "The Flea"); *Jacaranda Review* ("The Blood" and "Park Place"); *Lake Superior Review* ("Fat Lena & Mr. M."); *Light Year '85* ("Fat Lena & Mr. M." and "My Sister"); *Michigan Quarterly Review* ("Mnemonists," "Temporary Dwellings," and "What to Do While You're Waiting"); *Ohio Review* ("Tree in Autumn"); *Pig Iron* ("Squeaky Nursery Tunes"); *Ploughshares* ("Culmination" and "Let's All Get Up"); *The Ploughshares Reader* ("Let's All Get Up"); *Prairie Schooner* ("Perch"); *Radcliffe Quarterly* ("Brews," "Flocks of Phlox," and "Last Course"); *Small Chambers* ("Fat Lena & Mr. M."); *Southwest Review* ("Preference"); *Spazio Umano* ("Change" and "The Flea"); and *Tendril* ("Aging in April").

The poem "Catch" appeared originally in *The New Yorker*. "Let's All Get Up" received the Emily Dickinson Award from the Poetry Society of America in 1983, under the title "The Warrent in the Cloud." "Brews" received a Stroud International Poetry Festival Award in 1983. "Aging in April" received an Associated Writing Programs Anniversary Award in 1984.

*The publication of this book is supported by grants
from the National Endowment for the Arts
in Washington, D.C., a Federal agency,
and the Pennsylvania Council on the Arts.*

for Tama and David

CONTENTS

CONTENTS

TEMPORARY

DWELLINGS

LITTLE ELEGY

About our bodies there is much to know.
Imagine microscopic creatures who
inhabit capillaries, build cathedrals,
hovels, shopping malls. Who carry attaché

cases filled with radioactive dust,
scurry from New York to New Jersey,
"Le Coq d'Or" to "The Upper Crust." The fiscal
exchange is disease—half a pertussis

for a case of scabies. Frou-frou is
verboten: sadness, ecstasy, malaise,
not permitted. Violators will be
prosecuted, towed away, possibly

electrocuted on public TV.
Meanwhile, we, Gargantuan, take a taxi
to a chic masquerade wearing Mouseketeer
hats with our names appliquéd in silver.

We're having fun, maybe, not suspecting
that minute computers are programming
us to mirror, in the larger world we want
to think is ours, minuscule creatures. The sun

sifts through living room panes, paints designs
on our shining pharmaceutical cabinet.
We do not mind. We have enclosed ourselves
in waiting rooms with the blinds tight shut.

Or we are locked in the broom closet
between mops and floor wax, the feather
duster tickling our necks. Oh, we're sure
something is the matter. But what? What?

Our neighbor has a stroke. We don't regret
not knowing her. Our golden retriever,
"Little Brown Jug," topples over. A small
corpuscule explodes in his graying head.

We grieve for months, years, until our blood
is thinner than the thinnest gruel, until
the small bodies in the stream have disappeared.
Our grief is inexhaustible, peculiar,
a lingering fever we're left to live with.

4

COLE PORTER HAS
A NERVOUS BREAKDOWN

There was much hope: cops and robbers
racing in circles on flat, splayed feet,
a white efflorescence, lush puffs of butter

and salt. It was a strut down Main Street
doing the Lambeth Walk, the Fox Trot,
the Lindy Hop, the Conga for Madame

La Zonga—tops of thighs long
and limber over the cool silk run,
a widely paneled vestibule

furnished with swinging divans
for chirpings after the ball,
butter-brickle ice cream cones,

strings of beads, a party line.
After proms and flaming crepe suzettes
it was—it is—nostalgia time.

The price of all this fun? Someone
holding someone at the mercy, unshelling
the turtle, cringing the dog. Someone

two in the kitchen, watering
and salting the bouillabaisse, fingertips
red with scorch, the jangled horn of our

terminal cab coming to take us away
from this abyss of bliss—the heart a plucked
chicken clucking softly, "This is it. This is it."

ORPHEUS AND *LA DOLCE VITA*

Elect me president, why not, why not,
I promise you'll be driven in servile
limousines to watch croquet balls tumble
on unimpeachable greens. Your daughters
will cavort with cellos through mellow

afternoons, while you, reclining,
compose concertos on fresh hay.
This will keep your thoughts away
from mortar and from butter; when you
sketch with sticks on dusky walls,

depicting antelope and buffalo
lurching gracefully over nothing, no
piles of stock and venomous ilk
will coil in your way. I promise
each citizen an equal sum to write

lyrics, sonnets, and loony tunes,
to put a bee in every bonnet humming
in iambics; strophes and tropes adding
root and bloom will exude exotic
aromas in a jungle of golden freesias,

a garden of tropical fruits. My dear
brethren and sisters (I will say, raising
long arms as if to fly), do we not belong
to the same flock, all of us pariahs,
white and black? Once, fast asleep,

did I not awaken in a bed which rocked
like a ship going down, a rumble like
loose lions in the dark? The term
"earthquake," missing from my brain, by
its lack increased the residue of shock.

Oh elect me, if not president, then
present dick, then take stock and dead lock,
your local tic tic toc, tickets toc. If
I am elected we will play together
a game called the learning of names:

Porbeagle—a small shark of northern
seas noted for its voracity. Pooh-
pooh—to make light of. Trumpet-wood—
a musical tree of the mulberry family
with hollow stems and shield-shaped leaves.

Oh let us, benevolently, look after
the charges of that astonishing mother
nailed to the beak of the barque;
she has given us slippery words to tend,
squirming infants swaddled in vulture skin

who know nothing about political aims.
We can unwrap and release them
to seed in sweet water. We can train
the small minnows to swim. Ah,
we can do whatever we like with them.

WHAT TO DO WHILE YOU'RE WAITING

Of course it isn't wise to call attention—
is it a springer spaniel to come to your command?
Ordinary people sulk and groan, while you,
ethereal as an angel, must flitter and glide

if you don't want your breakdown known, also
must pare your eyebrows, resign your eyes. I've
tried. I've dusted *The Century* magazine,
bought a split-level colonial with a clipped

front yard, snap beans and garlic in back,
worn gardening gloves of black bombazine,
worked hard at imitating the stick
caterpillar, praying mantis, and other

cryptic characters. The children found me
out at last, tee-heeing and mouseketeering
as I hobbled past the Farmers' Hotel
and the bus terminal, throwing pebbles

at my retreating feet, dogs nipping my ankles,
ripping my stockings. Passion was my doing
and undoing, setting down guide lines
to trip me up: such records must be kept.

I've stuffed them under the mattress,
in the dishwasher, one or two beneath the stove.
I've been gentle, drying my heart, feeling it
friable as a dinner plate, then eyeing pieces

lying like a riddle on the kitchen floor.
Where's the help once hired to sweep up,
I wonder. I no longer leave the house. The spoons
curl in the knife drawer and the knives

have addled their way into the cat's box.
I know I must look after myself. Each morning
I remove my body from its quilt-cocoon,
careful not to slip the ticking of neuron

and vein. If I can love myself as I am
I can love anyone. I believe quite soon
my life will begin. So what if I'm seventy-three!
I've waited this long, I can continue this way.

I have hope! Any minute now someone named
Love will come prancing up my yellow brick walk.
Wearing a seersucker suit, a daffodil
in his lapel, and a straw boater,

he'll ring the bell. Hi grandma! he'll call.
I'll let him in. I'll let him in
saying, I knew you'd come. I've been
waiting for you, for my life to begin.

The door will swing open of its own volition,
the way an enormous rose unfolds its petals
and allows a honeybee to enter
the hot, fragrant chamber of the heart.

LET'S ALL GET UP

When your house is smashed by an avalanche,
and in the family room, where only minutes ago
you were watching General Hospital, you lie

moaning, crisscrossed with ribbons of wood
and wool, until hours later an Airedale
pulls you out by one ankle, do you get up

in the snow and tap dance? You know,
in a plaster cast from chin to toe, it's
not fun to sing Hallelujah. Unable to move

the tin man and I would make a fine team
if we could reach over, weave our twin
hands together. In the meantime, my feet

take root in the backyard dirt, the body
withers, my arms shed leaf by dry leaf.
Trapped in the interior a finch

beats bruised wings, as if it remembered
swooping down and ascending on a soft
current of air. Then the wind, the rain,

the mailman arriving from Barcelona to say
the children are fine. The travelers.
Flowering transplants dazed by the rough

tongue of the sun and the smell of tar
and the sting of brine. Oh casaba melon,
rind of lemon, flittering jacana!

It is not possible to forget.
From the bare branches of myself—
our house, our home— rising out of

chair legs and dinnerware, crumbling
rubble of kitchen and attic, ranting
rabble and riffraff of departmental

officialdom: declawed, hairless,
missing teeth, I smile, knowing that
somewhere in Spain, somewhere in Portugal

Hackensack or Poughkeepsie, they will see me
waving my fingerless arms
and they'll wave back.

LAST COURSE

It must have been my penance to teach the dead
cooking. Not that I was any good.
*Sing jig my jole, the pudding bowl, the table
and the frame.* . . . Their pitiless eyes
turned towards me. I was absurd. "Divinity

next time, darlings," I'd urge, sprightly.
"Read your books. Come with whips and spatulas."
I found them rather cold.
I think all they wanted was someone to love them.
I couldn't help them with that.

Under the weight of clothes, boxes, appliances,
the body—grasshopper arms and legs
sticking out—had fallen in the closet.
I could hear someone calling. Such disrepair!
The drapes needed cleaning. The dog whimpered.

My difficult duties were elsewhere.
I floated in a northwesterly direction.
Pâté sucrée. Marrons glacés. It seemed
these trifles were all I could imagine.
Candied petals on a whipped-cream sea.

It was hot as summer although it was spring;
budding trees were sabotaging the stiff
trees into motion. What about my creative
agility? They were certainly polite.
No one laughed at my frippery, my knivery,

my imperfect parfaits. I sighed when my time
was over, fitting myself once again into
that ailing chassis. Too tight around
the armpits, it was, and not to my liking.
I could feel my toenails turning purple.

Bafflements and trinkets clung to my ankles.
That's what life is about I thought.
Flummery, russes, tortes and tartes. Just desserts.
I look at cooking as a process, not a product.
But really! Soggy grapenuts in the chocolate soufflé!

I think of that time with shame, how I couldn't
open one student's eye to the Byzantine
glee of raspberry bombe or crème brulée.
I regard cooking as a religion, a way of life.
Salt instead of sugar in the icing!

PREFERENCE

This is a death without a death, with no
blue-eyed man blowing kisses at the dock,
no white ducks, fireworks, bouquets of hibiscus,

Pouilly-Fuissé on the rocks, no uncles
waving handkerchiefs, tears trickling,
dribbling babies held up to the sky.

This is a departure in shades of gray
paper with no one leaving. With one left
who lives on sprouts and dried bay leaves,

who wears Salvation Army sagging suits
with holes in the kneecaps and sleeves,
who spends hours and days applying,

appliquéing, cross-stitching and hatching,
mailing, sweeping, playing snip-snap-snorem
and bezique, opening bills—and bills

open, demanding nourishment. One
has none to bestow. One, left,
murmurs without a sound, "No. No. No."

Like the last passenger pigeon—no mate
could be found—who died, caged
and blind in a Cincinnati zoo, one claw

grasping an iron stand, one cannot
(one doesn't want to, one refuses to)
get used to this intensity of one-ness,

or accommodate this high
peak of uneasy
uniqueness.

WHAT WE WANT

1. Change

Certain Americans refuse to return
to the country or county of origin
fearing their roots will pull them

back into the soil, fearing the land
will cover them over, bright green
hairs like plastic grass in an Easter

basket will sprout on their private plots.
Where are our roots, Gussie's and mine?
Surely near some huge coastal mecca

mart, market, mall, bazaar, *sook.*
Gussie says, "Mother, perhaps we purchased
too much? I'm sorry about the checks."

Arms laden with parcels we take
a taxi home. Our feet ache.
The meter ticks: four   five   six.

We hear only the roll of breaking waves.
Gussie over-tips. My habitual glum
incantation begins: "Once again it's

plain you have no respect for the slim
thumbprints, the fibroblasts of skin
even small change is weighted with."

Gussie hushes up ferociously.
When I received my final decree
my father abstained from sustenance

for a week. "What will become of Gussie?"
He wept. No way for me to reply,
remembering how he'd walk sixty

city blocks to save a subway fare.
To ride cost a nickel then. Now
in our fashion, Gussie and I, warbling

mermaids, comb the snarls from our
raveled days. Sometimes we bring home
gifts for those who wait, round

soap on a rope, seals carved from stone,
seashells—each night fingering
findings like fat beads on strings.

Tonight we will sleep on the hefty
laps of angels. Tomorrow we will catch
a ride back to each store, the way
fortunate starfish return with the tide.

2. Anthropology

Gussie and I live by small clues
the way birds in the natural world observe
the web-markings of golden garden spiders.

Our friends are few. "Gussie," I say,
"You must learn to extend yourself."
"Mother, I am not a folding umbrella,"

she snaps. She refuses to respond at all
to other notices and rules such as:
"A lady of majestic appearance should

never wear white." Or, "It is vulgar
to stand with the arms akimbo."
She is enrolled in an evening school,

Lively Classes for the Intellectual Masses,
a course in anthropology; she reads me
bits selected from the text:

"In Swaziland the mahogany rat is driven
from the bush by brush fires
set by children. Emerging in agitation

he is clubbed to death by them. The skinned
carcass, sautéed with molasses
tastes sweet—not unlike chicken."

And a warning: "It is reported that a simple
sneeze can unleash an avalanche—rows of
frozen wedding cakes vanishing over a precipice."

We send out monthly invitations to musical
matinees—those who have taken part
may remain for *déjeuner*. For a five P.M.

family reunion a table set in the dining room
is supplied with tea, coffee, Melba toast,
and cinnamon buns, which constitute everything

offered to kin. Frequently I remind Gussie,
"Politeness is benevolence in small things."
Also, "Idleness—the source of misery."

We do not find fault or grumble but read only
books that uplift and instruct. Moral courage
is a rare endowment we pray for on our less

quiescent days. Gussie says, "Eskimos—charming
primitives—bundle their old relatives onto
ice floes, scoot them down cold rivers, looking brave."

3. Lodge Way

The question at breakfast: what to serve for
afternoon tea. Enchiladas? A salad is cooler.
Every speaker needs a listener. We have one

another—who speaks and who listens
is not always clear. Ms. Sunny Lay-Jaire
solicitous rehabilitator, will visit us

on Tuesday. Her duties with the elderly
keep her abysmally busy, an Olympic
skater dizzily exhibiting a hydra-headed spin.

She has plans for us, we must start again,
a new career, volunteer. Possibilities
lurch and beckon in the morning air, sprightly

enticements hung on a sagging line.
We might read *Gone with the Wind* to the blind,
cross-stitch potholders for deprived tribes. . . .

Our Cotswold cottage thermometer's peaking
at ninety-five. The T.V. is castrato.
A moth in the air conditioner has construed

a cocoon with a coarse biscuit-shaped wrapping.
Yesterday we were not unhappy, although nothing
was working, nothing was hatching. It was last

night's sordid struggle with sleep that left
our eyelids engorged, synapses out of gear.
We're slumped in a slough of corpuscular despair.

Everyone is young, rich, vigorous, except for
a few of us, too loquacious to be restless,
too hungry to be bored. Do try us again, dear

18

Ms. Lay-Jaire. How remorseful we are! We said
what we did, not meaning to be unfair or cruel.
What, after all, does an octopus know of ink?

Such an organism eats, sleeps and thrashes around
for its own, needy sake. We, having lived to accord
virtue its due, will not refuse a paltry reward:

three grapes. A cashew. A few wild strawberries
found in a patch behind the horse trough:
gritty, sparse—nearly enough.

4. Temporary Dwellings

Soon it will be holiday time.
Everyone will pay the gas bill,
stop the *Journal,* put Lulu and

Frito in a kennel, strap the baby
in his seat and take off for Greece
or the Appalachian Trail. Each year

we rent a place called Paradise.
En route, Tante Anna remembers
the broom that everyone else has

forgotten. We turn the car around.
At the far side of the Verrazano
when the sky is just beginning to glow

the mattress falls off the Subaru.
And the baby? Why ever is he screaming so?
The baby's developed intestinal flu.

At the bungalow no one has connected
the water. Mouse nests infest
the battered chests of drawers.

19

At last everything is set.
A few of us sprawl on the grass, chewing
on bile-green blades. Why are we not

rendered ecstatic by the supernal
world around us? Is it not summer—
too infrequent, these honeysuckle

days—hours dipped into nectar.
Ants come and bite our ankles.
The baby is stung by a bee—

After we've gone, someone will repaper
the bedroom and dust the rose leaves,
wondering, What were they like

the family who lived here? Perhaps
they played Patience, scrutinized
the constellations—named them—

Casseopeia, Orion, the Dipper.
At home, we discover our azalea deleafed
and deceased. Frito, the pinscher,

has acquired a bronchial wheeze.
He coughs until our hearts are sore.
Nevertheless, next year we'll persevere—

pack the car, forget the coffee—
with the repetitive buoyancy of a Vivaldi
refrain, or, more likely, "Amazing Grace,"

not knowing what disaster we are seeking
or dodging, the miles ticking past
from home to Paradise and back again.

5. Barter

Gussie is studying philosophy.
What can we, in truth, know,
touch, see, she asks pensively.
Of course, everyone wishes
to live in a free-floating pool

gently heated, only get out for
dinner: nubile jade asparagus spears
trembling like maids of honor
packed in ice, tulle bunches of
cauliflower flown in by private Lear,

while the rest of us wait for the snort
and snuffle of a mule on the horizon
hauling a box of wizened string beans
weeks old. In the sting of winter
when sky is dim and squirrels are

looking pitifully thin, rare
wildflowers of excessive beauty
may adorn the tables of the hoity-
toity beside the cognac and the tutti-
frutti, reason enough to be pish-and-

tushily snooty. Everyone forgets
that even the well-to-do must sleep,
dress, perform bodily ablutions.
Scraping the chin with tiny machines,
annoying one's skin with unguents

and creams, take minutes and hours even
for the affluent. Actually, isn't it time
we want, isn't it wanting we want—isn't
what we want the lie that truth is possible
if not achievable—the belief—however

brief and inconceivable—that somewhere
on some Elysian fields, men and women better
off than we—trilingual, carelessly regal—
are playing chemin de fer, sailing yachts,
dancing at discotheques and champagne balls
the old way, cheek-to-cheek, hearts parallel?

WHAT WE KNOW ABOUT
RIGHT-ANGLED TRIANGLES

One longs for unities, a cosmos
observing religious holidays. Countess
Maritsky woke one day with green half-

moon stains spoiling her negligee.
Is this unusual? The hue of trout
scissoring upstream against the grain

of water. When she and her husband,
the count, stopped their loving
business they were—how old—

fifty, sixty? Fortunate to suffer
only from amnesia. Yet his mourning
beard is still attached to his chin.

He smiles, conversing with blond
angels. She has an ecumenical
son, a civil daughter. It is summer.

Green caterpillars are eating
holes in the hems of roses.
A squared plus *B* squared equals

C squared, Pythagoras told us.
Life for him consisted of stiff
stuff and limber, imbued with

radiant numbers. He was a happy man.
Devout. Celibate. No one yet
has proved him wrong.

PERCH

Hausfrau! Barnacle!
What important or impertinent eye
makes you, tacky lady of the small-

petaled prints, afraid to mush
down to the vegetable stall,
afraid to mail your misspelled doggerel,

afraid to appear without your steel
needle-nosed pliers, ball peen hammer.
I, mother-in-law, shall teach you,

my daughter, what there is to fear:
let you lie in a nest of rutabaga,
put off until night the sunset

and recollection born in torn flesh
and matter. In torn flesh, a cold
fish from old bone and bladder.

The soup of stars begins to boil,
whirligig particles rise to the top.
Now streams the lantern into the lantern light.

Garrulous chickens will keep you awake tonight!
And, by the way, your neat hive of a kitchen,
efficient, yet so dangerous, with its mincers

and pincers, disposals and syringes,
whine of the microwave, grind of the processor,
the dish of cucumber yogurt

blended with grotesqueries and confitures
smashed on the floor . . .
I mull over gossipy eyes.

They crunch like celery when chewed.
Here's a mouth made of raspberry syrup,
dripping with lies. Drumstick eyebrows

streak into battle—a distracted
drummer lewdly cackles. While you,
at the oven, a frisbee-hatted Dalmatian chef,

roar and stew, fretting over your
addlepated sister, excessively peppering
the out-of-stock ragout—how can you,

late with dinner, stay here among such menacers,
and the mister, with his scowl, his scarf,
and his hairy arms due home at any minute?

THE FLEA

1.

Help help, help help
whispered the small creature
without clothes trapped

in the mesh of the strainer
I was stuffing spaghetti through.
With tweezers I plucked

him out, dressed him in minuscule
trousers, put a pair
of spectacles on his tiny snout.

We started a relationship
dining informally, in or out.
He sits on my knee.

He adores me, obviously:
pink welts from his kisses polka
dot my body. Such are the risks of

munificence and pity. Ah, pity,
bleak Vegas of hospitality!
He's become part of the family.

Can I ask him to leave?
He's bored, flipping about,
fingering his flute. I'm

the entire entertainment committee.
We'll go see Bruce Lee, maybe,
or "The Cabinet of Dr. Caligari."

I'll buy an ice cream after the movie,
double scoop, blueberry.
I lap such sweet stuff up.

He gets restless, waiting for me,
sticks out his thumb and hops
a ride home on our Weimaraner pup.

2.

So much energy in the mite,
zipping from a bewhiskered field mouse
    to someone sitting among us,
infecting us all with his wit, his flight
    high and wingless:

now layed out stiff
    legs sticking up
dressed in a tiny tuxedo.

This demise must be momentous.
Everyone's carrying something diaphanous—
    lacy gloves, careworn handkerchiefs.
Pipsqueak! I mutter petulantly.
    At my closing ceremony I will be

floored if there are three
    professional mourners.
Who is this rogue? Why such sobbing?

Outside, chauffeurs in livery idle
near lustrous limousines, pawing the ground
    with long leather boots, while
the eulogies in the chapel
    consume milleniums.

It takes milleniums to hollow
    caves from the stony
sides of cliffs facing the ocean.

    Only something simple as water
could change us this way.
    Around us our old zaddik pizzicatos,
sporting a leotard and black tutu,
    skinny as ever. And laughing,

laughing at us, paying homage
    our lives as usual
        swinish and short.

TREE IN AUTUMN

Expect me to bear your grudges?
I, who will not move, a homebody,
carry on 9 to 5, one hand spitefully

tapping its fingers, the other
tearing out tongues from the file?
Dolce! Dolce! In the fall

the light is too clear, the human
race trips at the wayside,
turns soft, shrivels.

Something new will slip into
the world, spotted and flawed,
neither machine nor fruit.

Who wouldn't look for a way out?
Few have been consulted, or given
three wishes, or one. I know

what must be done, although
the elements I have ingested
are weighted with millenniums —

will not recede from my veins.
The task requires a grace
a brown wren might possess,

or a cat stalking a wren,
pretending to be wooden,
planning to feast on a mess

of bones, flesh and feathers —
chassis leaning forward,
one foot lifted from the grass.

I am stodgy and humorless.
I had a purpose.
I am useless.

Compendiums of apples.
Wind sweeps the leaves.
Who will look after the people?

SQUEAKY NURSERY TUNES

The beans rolled and flip-
flopped when Jack's mother,
in a rage, tossed them
into the yard. But one
grew up to be a beanstalk,
a tough and gawky surprise.

Because we never do marry
English Lords the way we
were supposed to, or live
in the land of the bongo
drum with a mango moon,
a coconut sun, my sister
and I cut swastikas between
our eyebrows and dress in
shrouds. Calling ourselves
Dad and Mum, we jab each
other with kitchen forks.

The way I had a little
curl right in the middle
of my forehead, to hide
the line where they split
me exactly in two. With
their continual finding
of holes and stains, they
are sewn to my fingers still.

The way inside my head
smells of dead fish,
the way I am sitting
slumped against a wall

where dead flowers climb
up and up, clutching
a feathery clump of dust
and waiting for a beanstalk
to grow out of my fist.

WASHED UP WITH
MAXWELL BODENHEIM

Fish scales. Drying sails. Chilly
catcall of a gull. As if
a tornado, carrying
us a great distance, dropped us

into the lull like mailbags,
very angry, your eyebrows
crossed sticks, my voice breaking in
the middle. I love the way

your moustache curls into two
pale tails at the ends. You do
not see I notice the small
details of your body, a

broken eye tooth, your double-
jointed thumb. Unaware a
big toe is sticking up through
a hole in my sneaker, you

gaze at a reflection in
my sunglasses, the hazel
surface of the sea. We've both
lost track of our collision,

letters and leaflets slipping
through cracks in our seams, even
our names lost when the foam comes
too close. No one can leave here

until the wind picks up. What
I want to know is: the night
the bullet entered your skull,
coming as a shock, although

you thought yourself unflappable,
cool as an eel, in fact—
what was unfinished? Is there
anything I can do?

PARK PLACE

So, we are not to play with our puppets, then—
parcheesi games, tin trains, fire engines,
doll houses with families not like our own—
and the miniature dishes, pots and pans—
we are not to play with them, display them,
beat out our opponents at snip-snap-snorem.

We are not to feed the small stuffed lamb!
We're supposed to swivel around, saying,
Look at that, it's a rabbit, it's a drum!
Fat Lena, doll-soubrette, six hats and
a wooden rump. And a gentleman caller,
Mr. M. Look at her! Look at him!

The grownups will come and pack them away
for next year and the one after that.
But we wanted, we coveted—we remember
how much we lusted for—the roller skates,
the nested chickens, until our arms ached
and our tongues hung swollen with longing,

and the house a tundra where no iced
violets would sigh and revive, no dogs come
crying with joy at our arrival.

MY SISTER

After the funeral of her
husband, a lewd and filthy
inventor who dies leaving
her without a cent,
she dries her handkerchief
on the radiator and reflects,

"All I have left is my soul,
and, of course, my body, both
wrapped in the same thin paper.
Of the two, my body seems
more important, perhaps
because I'm hungry and out of
Pepperidge Farm and apricot jam."

Dressed in a magenta robe, her feet
bare, she takes the MTA to Harvard
Square, where she begins to hop about,
banging a tambourine, chanting,
Soul for sale! Sale on soul!
and other catchy slogans. But strollers
and joggers act as if her soul

is invisible as air or angels.
On the first day she collects thirty-
two cents in her begging bowl
and decides to sell her body instead.

VOICES

A downy gosling, Wally tucks
his head beneath his crooked arm,
tries to shut out the neon, the noise,
to nest within a nimbus of numb.

At night voices spatter him.
Days, beneath cement, the land
murmurs like an old man's minion,
he can feel its thick blood hum,

the grinding gears circling around,
the pistons pumping steel and iron.
Someone's become stronger than Mother,
he can't hear her restive whim

turn to a rice-rain the lackluster
wedding guests toss after him.
His bride's a willow for weeping, the roof
is leaking. Something must be done:

buckets set out to contain the sky.
His hair is slick with rain, the rain,
exasperated as an older
sister, hisses, "Why *did* you. Why?"—

saying he will take his death,
saying the earth will speak to him
again: he'll learn by rote and heart
the catch-all vocabulary of a growing dark.

KEEPERS OF THE FLAME

Division was what the children greeted
us with. Division and derision.
How bravely we went on. *Walk the dog!*

*Take out the garbage! WHAT TIME
DID YOU GET HOME LAST NIGHT? How late
can the library possibly be open?*

Absurd, the blue uncertainties
no seat belt can ensure. The wagging
tail of the Afghan rupturing a varicose vein

on the leg of the only available electrician.
The house a hangar from whence total strangers
landed and took off. The estuaries spreading

out like bowls of chicken broth. Well,
what is one to do? The children must
stay awake all night, snort cocaine, pass

SAT's, speak knowledgeably of tweeters.
Do they address us by our first names?
Then, let them eat the stinking garbage they

forget to cart away! Scavengers! Vermin!
There is nothing like a lack of appreciation
to make one remember what one will continue

to miss, and no thanks for that, eh?
Diadems of fatigue encircle their heads,
by now sparking into a brush fire

on the verge of wiping out California
and the state of Oregon, then to sweep
eastward through the northern Ivy Leagues,

everyone awake until dawn to guard silver
flatware and the twin Ming vases Uncle
Harry sent from Hong Kong on his last

business trip, to say nothing of our new
home entertainment center with video recorder.
Who is to pay for all this, we wonder?

With four of them remaindering at home,
breaking furniture, wearing out the hot
water, and no intentions of leaving—

the tax-sheltered retirement pension
guaranteed each hard-working, obedient citizen,
Martinique's gold beaches, piña coladas

in Venezuela, the lizardy terraces and florid
coves of Guadalajara—may never,
we worry, be ours.

PROGRESS

Most of the time the weight was on me, she,
stopping to rest or rust, filing her
nails with an emery board, bored, would not

agree to release him. True, he was
cadaverous before we let him go.
Why did she insist we struggle so

long, hoisting him up and up the mountain,
as if the conveyed conveyed something
unconveyable to the conveyers,

surreptitiously. He could no longer
change a carburetor or hang a
kitchen curtain. All that was over.

Nor could we remember whether he was
father or lover, with his crew cut and
camouflage suit—what year was it—or

did it matter—each year a variation
on the fugue of the one before, and
all such nasty tasks belonged to us, came

as if with our names on silver tags
chained to our ankles and wrists. It was my
idea to surrender him. I had

learned wait, and hesitate, and how to get
my own way smiling, humble, without
disparaging. Never disparaging.

Let us go left instead of right when
either side is wrong, living on freeze-dried,
the lining of my stomach cold as

wisdom. Nothing left to burn. Sitting on
the edge of this fissured cliff where he
fell or slipped from our conjoined grasp, we

might ask where are we to go, up where
the stars are melting and burgeoning, down
where the cows gorge on the forage of summer?

Why here, why not around elliptically,
or we might ask why are we

THE HOTEL PLUS LA MÊME CHOSE

1.

Outside, sprinklers spin in loops and arcs,
white orchids decorate the walks tended
by resolute gardeners. Everything's planned.

The starfish pond. Whistling swans in a cozy pen.
The sloping lawn has a view of the ocean.
We refuse to swim or lie down on the sand.

When we enter the dining room there's a hush
like the frozen shadows of cats
but no one bothers us or even comes near.

While the waiter, stiffly whisking
platters to and fro, bows, hovers
and directs a vain tableau.

We know how each event leaves an echo—
a bison sketched on a wall in Altamirra,
pebbles discarded from an Indian game.

2.

Conversation for two is often tricky
when one pair of eyes is rampaging about
looking for an exit out of this misprision.

Eyes like twin fish, wet and skittery,
sliding on the dish above the table.
Even the wine glasses crash,

the silver trembles in its rectitude.
The waiter will not venture from
his cranny behind the coffee urn.

The porcelain plates, rimmed with gold,
will last longer than we—pasty
with need, indolent in our lust.

3.

Between two minds, Safari Park, where
overweight lions slowly walk
as if they have thorns in their paws.

What use democracy
when we are chained to our rational chairs
when we should be out in the sun

plucking figs and hibiscus from green nests
or pulling up eggplants for dinner?
Jail must be more liberal

removing the necessity for courteous bowing,
tea table ceremony, a pinkie
curled like a shrimp.

4.

Our blood count is low, the nucleus
swells with those like us,
the fretters, the insomniacs.

In each room someone horizontal,
shutters hooked, an air conditioner spewing
a chill. Perhaps it is chemical,

this imbalance, the result of preservatives,
stabilizers, artificial dyes
dredged from nether regions.

Oh, but if once we could meet somewhere
other than this muted plateau, dispense
with routine responsibility, let

the center take over the whole—
if you would only look at me—would not
the moment come when those of us

43

lined up at the drugstore, prescriptions
for spansules and ampules with fanciful titles
clutched in our palms like small banners—

would not the moment come when we, who are
nothing if not sea creatures—japonica
and angel wings, cowries, violet snails—

would fling away our capsules, give up pretensions,
unzip our shells and float over the flooded hotel,
waking the sleepers from their bleak caves of salt?

THE SMALL LOAF OF AN ARTIST
IN SOCIETY

Two chihuahuas have tiny pillowcases
pulled over their heads with holes
cut out for eyes and noses.
Are they members of the Ku Klux Klan?

We do not know. Only, they must be
itchy in this warm dampness,
this summer sprinkled with peppery
flies over the ash cans of our lives.

What has blighted the stout cart-
puller, the homebody, the watch cur,
Beware of the Dog, a sign
leading to reticence in strangers.

All is changed, deranged and gone,
even slouches have a political
roll to fill. This is not a country
for old schnauzers or dull doubters

who muddle and fiddle and refuse
to remember the name of the street
they live on simply because they've
changed address once too often

and their furniture grows
molds and fungi in a warehouse
in Walla-Walla Washington. Changes!
Get used to them! some young rabble

rouser keeps yelling in the parking
lot on Twenty-Third Street, where
the organ grinder used to play
O Sole Mio just beneath the windows

of our mansion and his monkey tipped
his hat in mock thanks for the penny
that we threw him, although he cavorted
on hollyhocks and crushed petunias in

our Moorish garden, but it's too late
for giving an artist advice, who
having taken on the guise (gorge
and hackles) of a purebred dalmatian,
is polymorphous perverse now, indeed
always has been.

PÂTÉ

It is dinnertime, a dream of chicken with pin-
    feathers roasted dry: up and down
the domestic streets the strut of the rustic
    goose, the Sunday air thick with onion
soup and *pommes de terre frites.*

Something clear as oxygen is missing.
    The baby sings in his brief
crib, extending his range—flute,
    piccolo, high teakettle notes.
His quavery toes compose the air.

And I—what am I
    learning in my flat
box of a house, my head poking out
    the window, a huge, dull cabbage
waiting for the vegetable parade:

On spinach, on eggplant, come beet
    and kohlrabi, each hour is unfolding
like a cat named Wally
    stretching his bubble gum
mouth in a yawn, complacently kneading

and primping. His peignoir—orange fur.
    Weekdays, the ceiling hovers
over a rich feast: Wally in his bedroom
    slippers—plush velour lined with fleece.
Then the eye rises and its lush

imaginative ability pastes
    fuchsia trousers on elusive legs,
embroidering a scarlet dragon-jacket for what
    rises from the waist. Oh iridescent marmoset
benevolent above us, your focus glazed,

47

your tidy smile on reserve for overnight—
       a magic track circles you
on which our trains run late.
       Teach us Wally, hickory dickory, mouse
of a different color and clime, what

you know that makes the rest of us
       on any day, unnecessary.
Explain why, if I lie down, the yellow
       rug will cover me like grass,
like grease, the scum of boredom,

effluvium of apathy. I skim
       the gravy with a slotted spoon.
Is it the fashionable sexual
       laxity I lack, fleshly
exposures, etcetera?

Pick, pick. Pick, pick.
       So many of me, scolding, arguing,
I don't need a family, even
       on Sunday. All the bells in town
are clanging out of tune

and no bus runs. Formidable,
       this plain state of rest,
and someone beckoning from a petaled
       peak in the Pyrenees,
and me, too tired to ascend.

PARE

Spots on the fingers. Split nails.
Alien chemicals flush the corporeal flume.
We sneeze, but we are only two
people under one roof, inhaling
monoxides and insecticidal fumes.

Single-celled house guest! Pale paramecium!
We are not you although we inhabit
the same wheeling sphere—clearly
we are not divisible by binary fission.
Ours is the more convoluted, gloomy way.

For who can split the living room with
a feather duster or a blooming blue
wisteria spray? No separateness is more
unique than this wilderness, this
scalloped Swiss-chalet type bliss.

Magpie nests accumulate, dinner is pickled
in soot, farewell notes stick to the face
of the fan, the handle, slipping down,
clinks as the blades go round. Oh to rise
an inch, only one, above sea level!

So philosophers (you and I), unable
to escape the squeaking, squawking
wheel of the mind, push dull needles
through homespun cloth, prick our numb
fingers, unused to such tasks, sew

buttons on shirts never worn, or,
growing nimbler, embroider
rococo roses on silver kimonos.
What the surgeon does not dare to do
the sleeper rudely attempts, stitching

shattered ventricles and moonshine together,
winnowing chaos out of disorder.
Dust from a sticky dandelion hovers
in the morning air; the dibbling dawn
grows filmier, fingers its thin hair,

binding our two selves with flower wire;
but the limp green stalks are singular as
the stem of a daisy, a buttercup,
or a crimson love-lies-bleeding
just beginning to come up.

CONTEMPLATING MOTHER

1. My Mother's Cruise

Sitting in the convertible Pierce Arrow
his best friend tells her,
"My dear, he's looking for green.

Taffeta rustle of bills.
Patina of tended lawns.
Malice watered with silk.

And who is my Lady Greensleeves?
Not you, sweetie. And he's not the one
who'll plight your troth. He'll never sing

your baby salacious songs or rock him
in his crooked arms." Her hope sprouts
cinnamon spots, a kind of herpes

simplex of the heart. She longs to prove
him wrong. Studies have shown such a skewed
passion can demagnetize the moon, expel

serpents and sea lions from the sea,
the sea settling into wisdom, flat
and stale as a cow pond. "Mother," I said,

"Those photos, snapped so long ago, a slim
gosling girl holding daffodils, a lake
of slate-dark hair. Regard them as mere

fabrication, tweedle twaddle, to be cut
away with pinking shears. You ought
to glaze the sloop amazing blue,

tie red balloons aft. Do-si-do your corner
and allemande left." All that and more
I advised. But what could she do, just

close her eyes the way we children used to
in the House of Horrors, cuckoo cackles, jeers,
scalding lights, a mockery of nightmares

we willingly skidded and slid through?
Later, forgetting our fears in a rich
cream of epinephrine, we'd jabber

like a band of hell's sick angels.
We've given everything up, anguish
relinquished with hope, no more fixes,

how human we are we can't care. But I
reassure her, "Of course, something remains.
Something more and less than the body."

"I lack nothing," Mother tells me, "I have you."
Delight strokes her cheekbones with vermicular
tears before she dips down below deck.

2. Perspective in Gray and Green

She sends them off in a rubber boat,
bigger than the one in the bathtub.
"Here are oars," she says, "crackers,

water in a bottle, a stack of clean
handkerchiefs." They strap on
their jackets and go with haste,

growing smaller. Plankton leaps
through the waves of their hair,
their hair gleams in the sullen rain.

They shrink into two drops of water.
She raises her arms in semaphore
signals. They are too far to respond.

The cypresses weep with rain.
She turns her head not to see them.
She comprehends nothing of trees.

3. Brews

A pottery cow with milk in its middle moos
at the table. Once more a tin kettle whistles
and hops on a voluminous flame, a few women

settle around the mottled enamel rectangle,
their hands clutch the warmth of chipped cups,
butterfly lips hover primly on each brim.

Highland Avenue, is it? Stuffy apartment,
tufted sofa taking over, wooden ends
carved into cocoons. Whatnots, bureaus,

curios, cushions. Bones from the body
of memory, blood from old veins, case
mutable as moonshine. What's left is proof.

My doubtful, drabbled mother bending
over a shiftless daughter, crabby son,
barely notices the absence of fathers

or free floating men. She no longer hammers
the wallboard until the salt and pepper
shakers leap on their shelf in the corner,

no longer kicks open the bathroom door,
admires her nails under swirls of red lacquer,
no longer dabs her narrow ankles with jasmine

cologne or lavender. Under the delicate
skin of her wrist an insect quickens,
each night with the same dream: to reach

thin air, high altitudes, to become
a mountain lake, reflecting the stiffened
wings of hawks, accepting the sun, the rain.

54

Her smile is a flower, a white snip
she gives us, a snowberry at Christmas.
She begs for the truth, simple as a lily

or a white rose-mallow: her head,
is it slowly filling with snow, her feet
growing down through the floorboards?

Oh there are children, children, and the women,
thin and broody, enter the stippled room
like a procession of lit candles.

Their appetites huge with affection,
they aspire to pool in private kitchens,
flickering in corners, letting dog, cat

and neighbors in. Such refreshments taken
together may create, like the lotus,
a drowsy opus, a fugue of benevolence.

The room grows close, steamy as a tent.
The air hums with the scent of oranges
and cinnamon. For a moment my mother is able
to forget whatever it is she is missing.

4. Thin as a Nickel, Edgeless

Each year she dwindles, a wisp in a huge apron,
burdened with the weight of abortions,
beatings, thefts, whatever we are

up to. She's supposed to advise us, be
our working oracle, lay down sentences
like bricks, build walls, houses, steel

skyscrapers to protect us from accident
and erosion. Her eyes are so old it
hurts us to look at them. We know

we've told her more than we wanted,
worn her thin as a nickel, edgeless.
Nickel words, nickel eyes, nickel

old body dropped in the slot.
We're dancing to her music
winding down.

5. The Blood

My mother, skittering about,
little oxygen to speak of,
or with, in her veins: lips,
gums, cloud-pale—on an unruly
day her dull cheeks replay
gray tints of the sky. Nothing

slows her springy soles up
or down from her prestissimo
pace: run, work, shop, cook. *Go!*
Oh, I think when she and her sister
were children the air was purer
and the goulash and paprikash

they consumed with dumplings
no bigger than a thumb, all
in a piquant, savory sauce, and
the kipful and pugachel—such
succulent edibles—had nutriments
no longer in existence. The children

bloomed like prickly broom and yellow
gorse and had strength for the most
picayune, necessary tasks. Now
her sister, my favorite aunt,
a wraith with a lace-paper face
receding into Intensive Care,

tells the nurse, "Do what I want
or I'll roll up in a blanket,
lie out on the cold, hall floor."
The nurse does as she's told.
My aunt, minuscule, anemic, eighty-four
years old, a terror, *molto* bravura!

57

What happened in my case?
Stuffed with custard and cream
I'm buttery as a bird in
an expensive pastry—cowering,
terrified—a sitting pigeon—
with bones and a heart easily broken.

6. Catch

Scuba diving in the green murk
of Fiddler's Creek, our siblings
enjoy the bliss of fishes, cavorting.
Are they not the same species:
Gregory, Polly, Holly and the holy
mackerel? Water babies all and each
one dives to trawl a bigger finny
traveler with tinnier scales.
How Mother will adore whichever
offspring has the biggest haul,
she can fry it for supper.
This frolicsome lurching and
mauling, does it begin at birth?
At first, no one is hurt.
Later on, the sport is extended
to shark, barracuda, stingray:
leaky yachts sail the waters off
Key West, Florida, and the sun
breaks down tender tissue.
It is only after years of exhortation,
"Take an umbrella, stay below, swab
the decks," with the last sentence
nearly through, Mother whispers,
"Who's hooked now?" wiping pink
foam from her lips.

7. Aging in April

i

I was befuddled as a duck with wide, splayed feet.
My equipage was neat.
My hair was not.
                    My hair
was sizzling and black.
My mother would hold it back
with her hand, to free my bland face.
A haircut made a house of it.
Pitched roof, shingles,
                    dark shades drawn.
Go away! No one is home!

A sticky mist webs the ground
in the morning
                    ticking with silence
a wimpled figure grips the garden shears.

What is the point of clipping
those nearly invisible wires
that connect us,
                    the ultimate
network illusion.
                    Why not stop this
snip snip snip snip returning
each year like the blackberry bushes
eating the back stairs
                    Mother clipped after
Father died . . .
                    the next summer
lacked blackberries, and the stairs rattled.

60

I said,
    "You should sit,
sit on the front porch
staring at the bare fields of winter
                until your gaze
becomes clearer and the thumb-high grass
            is tufted with clover."

"They were going to strangle
the back stairs," she claims.
"You wouldn't want that!"

"But I asked you not to.
I said you could trim
                anything
but the blackberries!"

"I'll never cut anything more.
I'll never visit you again!
I found the clippers we bought
lying outside, rusted.
                I asked you
not to leave them out!"

We are branches, waving our arms.

My father built new steps
when the old ones rotted.
                We watched him
saw and hammer them in place, then paint
them white
                with flourishing strokes.

My mother still looks after him.

Wild blackberries should be forgotten,
left to grow
                    unkempt in profusion,
Cheap, cheap, a pocketful of rye, sing
                    the spring sparrows,
blackberry brandy,
                    blackberry pie.
We shall busy ourselves with abundance
in August,
                    picking quickly
before the birds strip the thicket.

ii

Her unmade bed is a bog, a swamp;
a white morning glory
                    she lies among the ruins.
Her eyelashes on the white pillow
have grown longer in a day.
                    She should be in order now—
hair mown and clipped
                    sheets pulled back.

I want a procession of tulips,
black and white, Indian file,
checkerboard style, a lawn party
with glazed cakes
                    and silver teapots,
my mother wearing a hollyhock hat.

She sleeps, or pretends to, but
I notice her face getting wet
in spite of the dry season.

My mouth hurts—as hers
where they have cut it,
cracks of blood stain the ends.
The sun's imposing even here

with the windows closed
against the noise of construction:
outside everything expands,
                they are driving posts
bringing pipelines into our heads.

All day we doze, sharing
a blue haze of contusion,
a flutter of pain-dulling pills,
walking in gardens
through rows of lobelia
and daffodils, tall and straight,
the way they used to grow.

iii

The chopping stops, the shears remain
splayed on the steps.
                I hear an occasional
drone of a jet.
                In the backyard starlings
flock and disperse. Pigeons
conclude their solicitous musings.

My eyes continue to sweep the flat
shadows on the ground into
                    a hill of branches.
My hair rises in an electrified cloud.
No one is here to pin it back.
The garden's a fright,
                    a shower of pollen
thigh-high with weeds. Mother
you were wrong. Or right. It
doesn't (did it ever?) matter.

SOLILOQUY IN AN EMPTY HALL

Good things can't always be happening,
you know, that prize check you expected—
through some vested fool's futility—

may have been sent to your brother,
your garrulous lover may never have
another word for you, although

you're wearing your spike-heeled boots
and your black mohair sweater from Peru.
Even now he may be telling his friends

you're an underripe neophyte such as
he has never seen the likes of—
if you heard him you would slowly rise

and settle, rise and settle, in your
wounded opposition to grievous gravity,
all your sugar coating would fall

to the floor and crunch under your heavy
landings, while the march of the sugarplum
fairies stuck in its groove until doomsday.

He comes. He goes. You de-petal a rose.
He is the sand crab. And you?
No one knows. No one knows. No one knows.

And your insomnia—oh let us not
speak of your hourly forays about
the dark house in search of anchovies

on toast or other sustenance or
release. How hunger at 3 A.M. begets
a biblical procession. Somebody who cared to

could name names, i.e.: peanut butter
begat jelly begat twenty-five Wheat Thins begat
milk begat a corn muffin begat a cluster of

M&Ms begat a cigarette-butt begat his
head on your . . . But what are you
begetting and what might be begat

by such beguiling begetting should you
begin in such a setting, a setting meant
for settling in? The drowsy quilts

you're nestling in are made for
indefatigable sin, and you
can't sleep alone. This may continue,

get worse as you get older, when
what's beginning is called winter—
chill fog between your sheets,

no more strawberries and grapes—
power failures, frozen pipes.
There are compensations for blood

gone thin. It's your birthday again.
And you—oh Admiral at the most
barbarous Pole—have been given a hole

in the ice, a black rubber suit, a tube
for breathing, and equipment for scouting
about in the frigid Northern sea. It's too cold

to stay down and live—a minute is what you have.

COMPOSITION OF A WINDY KNIGHT

After I squeezed behind your freezer
to tattoo my name on your palm
while you were asleep—after

I'm gone do you think
you will forget me?
I am taking my pythons, maps

and eagles. And my long needles.
And my box of dyes. And, yes,
my most effortless

melodious sighs. At Governor's Island
in the sixties, tattoo
used to precede taps. I'd compromise,

play both together and cross
the bay before sunrise. About
traveling, I have always been wise.

Any town such as this has an animal
sanctuary, a cemetery, and a few
humanists willing to pay for art.

Darling, no one can outsmart me.
My teeth are too pearly,
my mushrooms too libidinous.

Beneath crooked moons, mermaids
shuffle, by design, tarnished
spoons and cracked hearts.

I have grown expert at tombstones.
I no longer unpack mothy cartons
and cases. Bills spread disorder

over the floors, a tremor jars
my single bed. Unsteadied by such
shaking, I make ready to depart.

The fog horn blows and there's
no body of water, only night fires
keeping the town aglow, removing

the necessity for swine shows
and turkey shoots. Each day
deliveries are slower, the cats

are skinnier, another
crate is sealed. I cart plastic
sacks to the Goodwill box

and throw away my address book.
The clock has been defaced
by numerous droppings; springs

cogs and screws are lewdly
visible and the alarm is nearly
inaudible. The goose is cooked,

the wild swan has sung,
the great apes are nesting.
The ferris wheel will squeal

to a standstill at the annual
carnival. I will not be on it.
This is my farewell note.

THE ADVENTURESSES

Insistencies of eyes but no takers.
No finders. No keepers. They must, alas,
sail second class; while they are not failures

they suffer from *solitude à deux* which makes
them tremulous. Their suitcases are searched
and stripped. Darning needles fall from paper

packets into fripperies and slippers.
Lacy cases filled with bottles spill.
The cover of the Michelin has split.

Bald. They are bald. Wherever they appear
smooth skulls become *de rigueur*.
Purple crescents bob and dangle from their ears.

Their eyelashes are without color.
They are dressed in silver lamé,
the clinging skin of trout and mermaids.

It chills them, this risky venturing out,
although travel may reveal blue pickerel-
weed flowers on a second class table,

remaining home might have been less trouble.
It is March and cruel. It is not the cruelest
month. That has wastefully been taken.

They must stand in line for second place.
March marks my birthday, the former says,
I am the fish that swims in two directions.

They have learned the small death of hair—
turbans, ragged fringes, falls—
have passed through the mourning period.

Like some nearly-extinct, some flightless bird
they are so rare they are imposing.
The are so rare their composure is protrusively

well-bred. Amblers on the leeward deck stop
and say, "Hey lady, may I feel your head?"
Amused, they touch their nudity with cool fingers.

Such enormous possession! They tip with largesse.
The stewards are smitten with envy and lust.
You must adore water, they announce

to the former, seizing and stuffing her
through a porthole. Next time I travel
I'll take a tour guide with me, she thinks

morosely, before she slips off to garnish
the port-side depths. The last filaments of light
weaken. The wind's fee-faw-fum becomes a whine.

Staring from the railing at a glum horizon
the latter continues her crossing with a frown.
Must she endure *solitude à deux* alone? Even the thought
of shark-fin schnitzel for supper does not make her smile.

FAT LENA & MR. M.

The young girls flit and flutter, trying
    to brush the cold from the house,
they cut his hair, sew pink and purple pajamas,
    or make a set of glasses from old
beer bottles, the color of the sea.

But only fat Lena cooks, coq au vin,
    pumpkin soufflé, plum tarts topped
with nutmeg and cream, and the house
    smelling of garlic and cloves
and fresh bread rising and apples baking.

She watches Mr. M. as he eats,
    becomes a crumb dancing on the waves
in his mouth, slides
    down his throat and licks her lips
with a rather thick tongue.

Mr. M., O eat me too,
    she sings at the stove,
I will be married in the fall.

The dog barks at her shrill voice
    but he loves
Lena and the crisp skin of roast duckling
    she feeds him, basted with oranges
and ginger;
    and sometimes the delicate
                  fromage gourmandise
that Mr. M. brings home
    for his favorite dumpling.

As he nibbles her apricot ear Mr. M.
     is so safe from the cold
because fat Lena is the winter
     for him now and snow

the melting point of her white skin
     in front of the fire as she licks
his fingers as if they were
               lozenges,
   and he slowly devours her
       like a giant white
               wedding cake,
     topped with pink roses.

MNEMONISTS

Scotch tape on a scratch?
In this case it won't heal.
The platelets look
normal in color and design,

yet the bloody losers bleed
until . . . It takes time.
It takes an ability, a certain
quirk of the brain.

An aberration of the synapses?
A sex-linked mutation?
Even now, laboratories
run tests, compile information.

Startling results are forecast.
In the drafty treatment room
no transfusions will alter
the torsos, no hair

cover bald skulls. A familiar
eyebrow, a thumbnail,
a chip of bone may cause
bleeding to begin again.

Shameful! Willful!
Selfish! How the victims
smile, pretending, pretending,
until one night they wake

from pretensions—the bed
is a sticky red cradle
in which they are choking,
in which they are trying to swim.

And always arms, thighs and knees
clinging to despair
as if it were
a horse with golden wings.

And if their disease is catching?
What if there is no cure? Only
a machine-like memory,
the skin puffy,

bruising easily, a gradual, painful
decline in vitality, the senses
attenuating, the soul pulling
in like a snail.

THE PUPPETEER'S PUNCH

It is undeniable: your stringy features—
while not refined, not piquantly aligned—
are whimsical. Splinters from your tindery
torso lie under my nails, hide between
fingers, puncture minuscule veins.
Glue catches my thumbprints.

In the kitchen among empty peach
baskets and pickle barrels I taught
you to speak, perched you on a tiny trapeze,
sang tunes to you in my tinny tenor
until we harmonized, teetering together
on a thin rope in slippery air.

You are whatever I care to possess.
No one listens to voiceless heart cries.
It is true if I set you on chair or sofa
you would quicken with wonder, memorize
sliding panels, tucks in tweedy sleeves,
rapid exits, complexities, when what

I desire is decorous privacy. My petal,
how you tumble and strut in full light.
You must be resigned to dust, a slot,
a stuffy address. There is too much
between us. Your eyes,
one open, one shut, one

tear beginning to form.
Cold crotchets. How long we have
hoarded them! Oh poor Pierrot,
paralyzed god of wood and woe
I carry stashed in my side
pocket for life. Are we not well-matched?

FLOCKS OF PHLOX

Found on riverbanks when the tides are low.
It is nothing easy to forget, Wild Sweet-
William, *Phlox maculata*. Pink? Violet blue?
"Indeed, the same blossom may even change
color perceptibly within a day or two."

The Field Guide no longer necessary on walks,
although we were mere slips ambling across
the overgrown railroad tracks near Myrtle's Inlet,
when, turning to me (what cindery eyes you had—
the lashes, extra thicketed and furry) you said,

"All that shrubbery you are gathering—you look
like the African Serengeti we studied in geography."
It was true. I was radiant, a butterfly bush
laden with flora and fauna. My arms were
scratched from my elbows down to translucent

wrists where blue veins pulsed like cocoons.
In my sleeveless dotted Swiss I did heed
you then, and now you are underground and I
am sprightly in a drip-dry housedress.
Not that I'm having such a good time,

some mornings terror hustles me out of bed
with a forkful of lightning. Not that I'm
prettier. My body is lumpier and my teeth—
my wisdom teeth—are gone and others are bright
with silver; nevertheless, William, I am

footloose and nimble and you, who carved your
initials into my green heart, will never change
your purple-spotted stems, nor will we grow
wiser together. It is nothing easy to dismiss—
that small hole in what was once
a map of possibilities.

CULMINATION

The race is not over, yet the prize
beyond which no other exists
belongs to one of us; oh do not ask

what is it, is it voluminous, is it
exquisite, put your hand in the cloth
bag and draw. You too have been given,

or will be, a parcel of absurdity:
not half a diary, not last year's
calendar with a weeping farm girl

on the cover. Each prize presenting
no fiscal wherewithal at all, nothing
like that, each prize of the crudest

design and material, fitted to each
individual shoulder, armpit and thigh,
your reward for loping, loping

through fragile days and nights,
past tobacco barns, a goat and three
chickens, a landscape you have colored

with blue and green crayons a leaf
at a time. In one corner, a brown
house, smoke curling from a chimney;

behind red curtains uncertain faces
wait to be erased. The white dresser
with a missing knob will also disappear,

and the maple four-poster. You are
bedeviled as a cake, but dry, too stiff
to speak. Your lips are straight.

Have you been running your life for this,
for this? This lack of excess,
this nudity, bliss, this bliss.

PITT POETRY SERIES
Ed Ochester, General Editor

Dannie Abse, *Collected Poems*

Claribel Alegría, *Flowers from the Volcano*

Jon Anderson, *Death and Friends*

Jon Anderson, *In Sepia*

Jon Anderson, *Looking for Jonathan*

Maggie Anderson, *Cold Comfort*

Michael Benedikt, *The Badminton at Great Barrington; Or, Gustave Mahler & the Chattanooga Choo-Choo*

Michael Burkard, *Ruby for Grief*

Kathy Callaway, *Heart of the Garfish*

Siv Cedering, *Letters from the Floating World*

Lorna Dee Cervantes, *Emplumada*

Robert Coles, *A Festering Sweetness: Poems of American People*

Kate Daniels, *The White Wave*

Norman Dubie, *Alehouse Sonnets*

Stuart Dybek, *Brass Knuckles*

Odysseus Elytis, *The Axion Esti*

Brendan Galvin, *The Minutes No One Owns*

Gary Gildner, *Blue Like the Heavens: New & Selected Poems*

Gary Gildner, *Digging for Indians*

Gary Gildner, *First Practice*

Gary Gildner, *Nails*

Gary Gildner, *The Runner*

Bruce Guernsey, *January Thaw*

Michael S. Harper, *Song: I Want a Witness*

Gwen Head, *The Ten Thousandth Night*

Barbara Helfgott Hyett, *In Evidence: Poems of the Liberation of Nazi Concentration Camps*

Milne Holton and Graham W. Reid, eds., *Reading the Ashes: An Anthology of the Poetry of Modern Macedonia*

Milne Holton and Paul Vangelisti, eds., *The New Polish Poetry: A Bilingual Collection*

David Huddle, *Paper Boy*

Phyllis Janowitz, *Temporary Dwellings*

Lawrence Joseph, *Shouting at No One*

Shirley Kaufman, *From One Life to Another*

Shirley Kaufman, *Gold Country*

Etheridge Knight, *The Essential Etheridge Knight*

Ted Kooser, *One World at a Time*

Ted Kooser, *Sure Signs: New and Selected Poems*

Larry Levis, *Winter Stars*

Larry Levis, *Wrecking Crew*

Robert Louthan, *Living in Code*